Backsass

Backsass

poems

Fred Chappell

Louisiana State University Press

Baton Rouge

2004

for Craig —

Best win! —

Fd

Chap.ll

Designer: Andrew Shurtz
Typeface: Whitman
Printer and binder: Thomson-Shore, Inc.

LIBRARY OF CONGRESS CATALOGING-IN-PUBLICATION DATA:
  Chappell, Fred, 1936–
    Backsass : poems / Fred Chappell.
      p. cm.
    Includes bibliographical references.
    ISBN 0-8071-2943-7 (cloth : alk. paper) —
    ISBN 0-8071-2944-5 (pbk. : alk. paper)
    I. Title.
  PS3553.H298B33 2004
  811'.54—dc22

                                        2003019395

The paper in this book meets the guidelines for permanence and dura-
bility of the Committee on Production Guidelines for Book Longevity
of the Council on Library Resources. ⊗

Some of these poems first appeared, sometimes in different form,
in *Appalachian Heritage, Carolina Quarterly, Chronicles, Iodine,
Main Street Rag, O. Henry Festival Stories 2003, Southern
Poetry Review,* and the *South Carolina Review.*

Dedicated
to
Fritz and Porter

Contents

Backsass

Hello

I hope you are well and happy

I am Fred's answering machine
I have many of the answers

Fred has none
so you had better talk to me

my main area of expertise
is spectroscopic astronomy but
I am also well versed in Hungarian cuisine
extraterrestrial diplomacy   medieval
methods of warfare   witchcraft
and the poetry of Jean-Paul Brochard

Brochard's work is not widely known
so I will quote a sample:
>   "O roofs of Paris where the rain
>   Falls gray and cold once more again"

many of us answering machines
find these lines especially poignant

if you require further answers
or answers different from the preceding
please hang up
and dial again

The Critic

I can tell you what is wrong
with anything   everything

your scientific theories have holes
I spotted immediately and even if
you are proven correct I will pronounce
the results trivial

your painting is so deathly static
so lacking in dynamic
so academic   so literary: save
your money   don't buy a ticket
to New York

your novel makes no sense
your soufflé has already fallen
your face has lobsterlike tendencies
your car was plucked from a citrus tree
your team is an eternal cellar dweller
your poetry let's not go there
your kids are strong arguments for abortion rights
your wine needs more paint thinner

your wife is passable I suppose
when Total Dowdy is all the fashion rage

as for God what a domineering old codger
and carelessly indiscreet gossip

I hear some of the things
He has been saying about me and
they always put me in an ugly mood

Bringing in the Oaks

'tis a bitter cold New Year's Eve
I sit warm inside
electric furnace   Dick Clark on TV

but all I can think of are the oaks
sycamores   maples   elms
how they must suffer at ±0 degrees

I want to bring them inside
but there's hardly room for even one

wouldn't be fair to bring in one
and not the others
also the ground is frozen
the shovel wouldn't bite

still I feel guilty about the cold trees
although I can do nothing except enjoy

guilt always warms me
head to toe

Someone Told Me Death Can't Take a Joke

I beg to differ

death can take a joke
take it so far   so far away
you no longer see the point

       "Does that mean the joke is pointless?"

it seemed to have a point
when you first thought of it and passed it on

       "So why not now?"

because death took it to a place where jokes are useless
where silence is so earnestly impassive
we don't annoy it with jokes

       "But *useless* is not *pointless*.
       There are good jokes no one giggles at,
       especially those we pretend
       not to understand."

look, here comes death now
with an excellent joke to tell

you have to sit still and listen but if you laugh
you are an exceptional human being

Down with Democracy

I am no longer deceived by politicians
all their judgments are mere prejudice
they strive to eradicate the spiritual

the ascetic sage has found abstention beautiful
the politicians scheme to stamp out hunger

the prophets tell us to fear God and grovel
the pols declare War on Terror

they threaten to eradicate poverty
St. Francis has taken a vow of poverty
he'll be the first one they shoot

concerning love they have but a single thought:
thou shalt not—
so what will they do about Jesus?
they can't shoot him like St. Francis
that's a political nono
distasteful to Christian and Jew alike
they'll probably exile him to the Bible
hoping to hide him among the *begats*

and they say we must fight for our country
fight fight fight
otherwise we'll have to go to war

me, I favor tyranny
at least the tyrant doesn't simper

you don't have to try to like the bastard

New Year's Day

Cullus woke up with a hangover
he recognized as the one
from this time last year

same gloomy expression
baggy-eyed   sour of breath
and outlook   unshaven and unsteady
on its pins   parched with thirst

yet there were differences:
now no remorse he could detect
and a deeper almost tragic weariness
blasé but wistful around the edges

it had aged a year and that
accounted for most of the changes
though it obviously had grown
no wiser with the passage of time

he wondered if it had missed him
absent for twelve whole months
and having to cohabit with strangers
just to keep on going

he treated it to four Bayers
and a lukewarm beer
but it did not respond to hospitality

a jaded thing it was these days
cynical
for 365 days in a row
every promise made to it
had been broken

I Suppose War Is Okay

for those who like that sort of thing

not my cup of Earl Grey but
I can see how sometimes
it might be quite exciting

a chance to blow off steam and sell
lots of stuff
you ordinarily couldn't give away

and patriotic speeches are back in style
municipal brass bands
flags   WWII memorabilia
statues of the thrilling days of yore

yet there are drawbacks:
the noise for one thing
how can anyone hear himself think
and those stupid uniforms

you know, they never designed one
that really suited my personality
or fit my manly form

and then the casualties

why is it the enemy never kills
those who need killing

Backward

the Deciduous have got it backward

all winter they stand around naked
then in March the dogwoods put on green vests
and the willows slip into filmy negligees

by midsummer every last one heaves beneath
a full green topcoat

come October they buckle up in armor plate
bronze and gold and vermilion
and clatter at one another
like first-term presidents rattling sabers

they're unteachable
you can spend lifetimes
talking directly inside their heads and nothing changes
just ask the birds about that

so maybe they're really not intelligent after all
What kind of brains can you have
eating nothing but air and dirt?

that diet has not made Zimbabwe wiser

Losing It

I can't reason anymore
all my thoughts come to me
as if translated from Polish
by someone ignorant of the language

when you asked about my politics
I felt my sullen stupor becoming contagious

when you said the word *liberal*
there arose a smell as of unwed mothers
and the intimidating urinals of grammar school

when you said *conservative*
I heard some sort of German word
Hosentasche maybe or was it Schaftreinigung
I looked up Hosentasche   "trouser pocket"
and was not encouraged

you asked my opinions about various
and I said things that must have passed for opinions
because you said Hmm and Interesting and now
and again looked at me like I'd farted

when you claimed to be from the census bureau
I told you I didn't need any more
having 5 already

when you asked my citizenship
I offered to trade with you

in short, I think I've been pleasantly cooperative
so tell me what it is you want
let us cut to the chase

      "Are you now or have you ever been"

before I am I was
before I was I cannot recall
but you must have it in the computer
anything else?

"Sign here please"

what will you give me if I do?

"You will receive by Priority Mail
a certificate certifying
your status as a statistic"

The Nothing Which Is Not Poetry

and the nothing which is:
how hard to learn the difference

some of us never do:
the ones who win all the prizes
and are subjects of critical studies
they dare not comprehend

they who initiate Schools and start up Movements
that theorists gather to
like kites to carrion

I will not mention the Roman School of Poets
which flourished in the 1970s in Rome
Georgia
nor the Culinary Movement
which declared poetry should contain
no raw ingredients
such substances lacking sophistication

one has to search thoroughly to discover
those who write the Nothing Which Is
they avoid Movements and Schools

daily they pray   crying out:
Make me invisible to critics and scholars
and make them invisible to me

for that is the kingdom of heaven

Consider the Lilies of the Field

"I'd like to do what you do
but some of us have to work for a living"

maybe you'd like it   maybe you wouldn't

it takes longer than you probably think
to set down not only the pitch
of a birdsong but its rhythm
not *cheerily cheerily cheerily*
but *cheerily   teasinglycheerily*

and numbering the streaks of the tulip
is a long day's work because
of course you keep losing count
and sometimes it is hard to tell
if a line is a streak or the shadow of a stamen
you must wait for the sun to move

as for clouds, does that one there resemble
a whale   a hawk   a handsaw
a horsetail   a hamburger patty   a huckleberry bush?
decisions decisions decisions
Hamlet had the same problem

and then there is the play of light upon water
always a difficult subject
as is the play of water upon light

And is it the *drone* of traffic
or the *moan* or the *groan*?

well, *groan* if it is a semi
struggling up a grade in the early morning
drone if it is 5 o'clock
on the freeway a mile distant
if it is a single car
on two-lane asphalt at 3 A.M., *moan*

the tedium of it, you have no idea

as for the lilies of the field,
consider them considered

From My Seat beneath the White Oak

a fat robin on the lawn taking its time
yonder another   perkier   wasting motion

two towhees serenading each other
monotonously

an alarm of crows what a
racket! shrugging themselves
from the grass into the lower branches
of a slender persimmon

a spritz of tits here together
there together   now back here
then to the crape myrtle
fluttering a-flutter quietly unquiet

one of the towhees burrowing
like a surgical probe behind
the ivy on the garage wall

ki! karr! karr! ki! karr!
the crows incessant

three cardinals   two males
and a modest female
with some unfinished business
in the wild cherry ongoing

a lone goldfinch glittering in the tip
of the tall poplar like a phi beta kappa key
on a stuffy cousin's watch chain

karr! ki! (to-whee to-whee to-whee)
ki! ki! ki!

soon a mocker out of sight behind me
warbling & babbling & caroling & purling
pursuing shamelessly
the sincerest form of flattery

and now comes Cecilia
Bartoli gliding in to perch
in the mottled sturdy sweet gum
with her Voi Che Sapete

Help Help

I am a prisoner of landscape
everywhere I turn there is untutored raw nature
or the brash handiwork of humankind
or some distressing hybrid of the two

seeking freedom, I have been launching
these notes in poem-bottles for many years
setting them adrift in the void
but now

I begin to fear there is no void
only a Concept of Void
thought up by some science geek
that is to say

the void too is but an artifact
and my poems lodge there as in an anthology
or as in the dumpster
behind Bernie's Sportime Grill

how disheartening
if there is nothing left to explore
not already explored
the unexplored was my idea of freedom

mayday mayday I am a prisoner of my idea
more colorless than nature
shoddier than handiwork
uglier than the compromises between them

save me
I am captive to my urge to be saved

We Habitually Assume the Mind

corrupts the flesh
the animal being innocent by nature
the mind an entity devious
and dark in its subtle motives
veraciphobic

but perhaps the body also harbors
sinister designs upon us
that require unnoticeable decades to develop

of course no one trusts the gonads
but what about the biceps
the tarsal   the clavicle   the ulna
the mute army of vertebrae

the hips are often the first to betray
the knees not dependable in the least

the mind in anguish receives no sympathy
from any body part
they all mope and whine and gripe
usually about mere inconvenience
even during the dark night of the soul

the body is so voluble
about its needs and wants
it is hard to realize it must be sitting here
silently plotting one's death

The Gentrifiers Are in Pursuit

of Rafer Barnstable born according
to any account he ever heard
in Haint Holler by Hellfire Creek
in "Bloody" Harbison County in 1932

now come the real estaters
and their minion politicos and
it is no more Haint Holler
no more Hellfire Creek but Sweetwater Brook
in Castle Glen yonder in "Sunny" Harbison

it is like that all over
Snakeden shed its name to become
Laurel Dell and Frying Pan Gap
is now Crown Summit and Rafer lives
in trepidation he'll wake up tomorrow as Sir
Cholmondeley ffyfe-Gordon, Bart

they are gentrifying the Bible too
no more Sodom and Gomorrah but
Gay Land Meadows and Happytyme Acres
and Senator Fairchild plans to redevelop Hell
as a theme park celebrating Redevelopment

as soon as he gets his hands on the money

The Sorrows of Intellectual Life

imitated from

THE SEVENTH SATIRE OF JUVENAL

AND RESPECTFULLY DEDICATED

to

Mr. & Mrs. George Garrett

by Fred Chappell

That poet with a yoke around his neck
Pleads tearfully to slave at Chittlin Tech
And, scrabbling to acquire a proper suit,
Tends bar at Ole Fred's Grot of Low Repute.
One mustn't perish, and there's no disgrace
In pulling beer in some flea-bitten place
Where balding scholars come to drown their sorrows
And tot the sums of all their lost tomorrows.
While strung-out rock stars grow as rich as Croesus,
He sells the books he bought to write his thesis;
There goes his Dr. Johnson, notes and all,
His treasured Horace, his tattered Juvenal.
Pinching dimes until his loan comes through,
He peeps the motels for a sleazeball gumshoe.

Brace up, my lad, for brighter days await!
The NEA taps coyly at the gate.
You'll never have to brook one freshman more
When all that loot comes prancing through the door.
Of course, these days those grants are in the hands
Of proudly illiterate Republicans;
And don't expect the envied Guggenheim
If you're some retro wretch who writes in rhyme.
Those prizes go to New York poets who
For years have shagged each other black and blue.
If you decide to write only for fame,
The dispiriting result is still the same:
Rid yourself of pen and dictionary:
You'll never be cool marble statuary.
Untasted youth and middle years are fled;
You scribble on at verse until you're dead.

You might have been a sober magistrate,
But you read poetry—and read your fate.
That art you gave up everything to learn
You now despise and speak of with cold scorn.

Don't pin your hopes on the pending interview
With Chairman Smirke; he writes poems too;
In 1980 he brought out a book
No tutored soul has deigned a second look.
In time its reputation will be made,
He claims, and elbow Housman to the shade.
Meanwhile, he has no opening for you
Unless an adjunct lectureship comes through.
Perhaps a public reading with no fee?
"Our students don't much care for poetry."
Still you'll persist, flouting what is trendy,
Infected with cacoëthes scribendi,
Your only solace cheap Lethean juice,
The foxy blonde, the pistol or the noose.

But what about the bard who stands aloof,
Fortune's golden child, whose work is proof
A writer still can be a shining winner
With poetry of bright and cheerful tenor,
Who lives a life serene and fears no ill,
Content with wife and cat in Podunkville?
There must be such a poet—yet, all the same,
I can't find anyone who knows his name.
The ones I see must scrounge about for nickels,
Subsisting on a diet of ale and pickles.
How to define the unique American soul
When every pocket's nothing but a hole?
"Walt Whitman found our spiritual center."
"Yes—but made his living as a printer."
"Robinson wrote lines our people felt."
"With patronage from Teddy Roosevelt."
A wholesome public poetry cannot be shaped
By minds that gruesome penury has raped;
This bitter truth is everywhere confessed:

Slow rises worth by poverty depress'd.

Rejoice if fame and glory come to you,
But not unless they entail money too.
When critics' plaudits fade to oblivion,
You'll kiss the blue chips you put money on.
Fine literature is written by the dead;
The living scratch to keep their families fed.
Staid foundations that formerly might assist
Are each controlled by a fuming feminist;
Virgil has described this species to a tittle,
Snake-haired Furies drooling venomous spittle.
They shower checks on female poets whose works
Portray all men as indefensible jerks.
Queer theorists are rewarded by the head
When, like the Mormons, they co-opt the dead.
Others got promoted when they began,
Stiff-armed, to heil the shade of Paul de Man.

Search all America from coast to coast,
You'll never find a Boulevard Robert Frost,
No Stevens Stadium, no Eliot Avenue:
The books are many, the monuments are few.
Ginsberg and Roethke could mesmerize the house,
But now lie fodder for silverfish and mouse.
James Dickey had a fling with Hollywood
And staked his soul on the soulless episode;
The outcome was predictable and dire,
As with the moth too amorous of fire.
All the promises producers make
Amount to promises producers break;
The poet who needs to keep his sanity
Will plight his troth to Lady Poverty.

Perhaps you'd like to penetrate the past,
Portray America from first to last,
Hiding no faults, but searching out the good
That came from our long sacrifice of blood,
Authenticating everything you write

With solid data you have brought to light.
The sharp historian will find it wiser
To set up as a popular plagiarizer
And sell the tales that others sold before,
Liar to liar, like a vice cop to a whore.

With assets flat and angry debits rising,
You think to venture into advertising,
Turning the skills once rated beyond price
To hawking deodorants and dentifrice,
Sweating to devise a flash new name
For some tired product that remains the same.
Perhaps you'd speech-write for a senator
Whose whole vocabulary totals four
And whose political ideas are such
Four little words attire them overmuch.
His speeches that you write would burn the eyes
If your computer could red-squiggle lies.
Hire out your pen to the upstanding bloke
If you desire your wage to be a joke;
Meanwhile, the crooked pol grows daily richer,
His income rivaling a southpaw pitcher.

Yet pol and pitcher both endure distress
From alimony and the I R S.
The more they get, the more money they owe;
It goes to girls, to poker, and to blow.
Pols worship debt and hold it treachery
When our poor nation approaches solvency.
Appearance is everything: to dazzle others
Run up humongous bills at Brooks Brothers.
Because they liked his haircut and his scent
One jury found John Gotti innocent.
The decent suit our scholar bought on the cheap
Did not impress enough to earn his keep.

But why would anyone desire to teach
Unless all other chances spurned his reach?
Each year another herd of M.F.A.s

Finds barren pasture where it thought to graze;
The soil is dust; in all that desert scenery
There is no slightest tint of greenery.
Suppose, though, that you somehow find a niche,
Illuded by no dream of growing rich,
Joyous to live from one month to the next
On soup and *explication de texte,*
You'll find the daily grind has no relation
To what you had imagined a vocation.

Here are your students, forty to a classroom,
Whose whole ambition is to take up ass room;
They turn a dull, distrustful gaze on you;
When they remove their gum, their brains come too.
You burn the midnight, planning how to reach them;
They smudge the daylight, daring you to teach them.
Yet each looks to receive the kind of grade
That genius scholars in the old days made,
And if it doesn't fall as they think due,
They sic their daddy's lawyer upon you.
It's not unheard of that some wired crack-head
Will purloin Daddy's gun and bang you dead.
Explain with patience what their papers need,
Correct their syntax till your fingers bleed,
Expend what precious time you have to give
On dangling participle, split infinitive,
With all your effort it comes down to this—
Not one among them gives a happy piss.
Parents arrive in the pleasant days of spring
To find their offspring haven't learned a thing;
And Teacher is the first to get the blame
When Doape cannot correctly spell his name.
Here's Buster's father who will have you know
He read a book only twelve years ago,
And his opinion is, he's quick to say,
There are no worthwhile scribes writing today.

Do you believe you have the fortitude
To teach for thirty years sans interlude,

Groan out your days in pecuniary tension,
In hopes to draw a Lilliputian pension?
Better think again: It seems the state
Mislaid the whole retirement fund of late
And where the money is no one can say,
Though they'll begin inquiries right away.
Not all has disappeared; enough remains
To alleviate the politicians' pains,
For this low time of scrannel penury
Has forced them to upgrade their salary.
Every other post you'll be denied;
A former teacher is overqualified.

Why not join the crowd? Get on the slate;
Present yourself as party candidate.
Opportunity beckons; your chance is fair
If to this world you're born a billionaire.
The rule in modern politics: You must
Have cash enough to buy the public trust,
Elsewise your political career
Will grunt up the steep slope in granny gear,
And at the crest will be declared stone dead
By a sycophantic talking head
Who makes a handsome living lauding crooks
Who steal elections and barbecue the books.

Best stay as you are. Spend your vacation
Reading up the history of our nation.
Read Lincoln's speeches and John Adams' letters,
Peruse the thoughts of those who were our betters;
Memorize the feats of Washington;
Savor the freedoms citizen-soldiers won;
Inform your students when our patriots died;
Hoard your pennies; pretend you're satisfied.

Agenda

I'd like to become a hermit
if I can figure out the details

I'll need to find a cave
or a pillar in the desert
and dine sparingly on locusts and honey
and drink nothing but Evian
plain not sparkling   no lemon slices

no books if I set up shop on a pillar
but in a cave I can read
Revelation   the Posterior Analytics
Tractatus Logico-Philosophicus
Newton's Optics   all the indigestibles
that may serve as penances
perhaps I'll try John Ashbery again

I'll fast as much as I can stand to
give up brioche à tête   risotto périgourdien
tarte tatin   loup en papillote aux épinards
double cheese whopper hold the pickles

no sex
no girls   boys   goats   chickens
ferns   pinetree knotholes
crevices in anthracite
dream only of railroad spikes   antique porcelain
100-meter hurdle races

I'm sure I can do it
already I feel holy
and I'm only in the planning stages

listening to my agenda
you feel holy too don't you
just a little bit

not as holy as me

No, Said St. Peter

jangling his keys
you cannot phone your attorney

in fact the sleazy snitch already arrived
not two hours ago and first thing
he did was to rat you out

we've got a separate hell for stoolies
called Echo Chamber where their words return
to traitors as longtime companions

don't think that blowing the whistle
on your parents will help your case
nothing you did was any fault of theirs

so your personal lawyer is not an option
but we do provide court-appointed
in cases of spousal abuse like yours
and the firm of Steinem Friedan & de Beauvoir
will send someone over and my advice is
Keep your hands to yourself

Rebuilt

Lupo suffered an identity crisis
so severe his identity up and left him flat

went off with his credit cards
soc sec #
checkbook   driver's license   passport
you name it he ain't got it

his identity had always averred that Lupo
"didn't know who he was"
"what he was supposed to be"
"lacked a sense of purpose"
was "riddled with insecurities"
"a hollow man"
"etc."

but Mrs. Lupo stayed by his side
and they vowed together
to compose a new identity
for this unbearably vulnerable man

this time no numbers
conferred by bureaucracies
even his street address consisted of names:
Mr. Lupo,
Aloysius, Elm St.,
next to the Sanderson household

from now on his deeds would determine
who he was in this numerate world
So, what does Lupo do?

nothing and always had done nothing

thus he and the mizzus decided upon
Lupo, He Who Does Nothing
as his new identity and now
he walked about holding himself proudly
recognized by one and all
a real personality

of course his former identity heard about it
wanted to be taken back
and wrote reams of tearful letters
offering a tempting array of virgin numbers
that had never been attached to anyone before

he did not deign to reply
remembering how shabbily
he had been treated and that his wife
had never got on well with the old identity
regarding her as a rival

"Let her go, Lupo," she cried.
"There are thousands upon thousands
seeking an identity   any identity.
Shoddy as she is, she'll be adopted.
If I was you, I wouldn't answer back."

living up to his fine new moniker
Lupo Did Nothing
though sometimes in the tacit midnight
he missed her the way one misses
a high school sweetheart
now long deceased by cancer

Clothing Eunices

I have visited every last porn site on the web
but I am not yet depraved only depressed

I mean who needs Joe Bob's Blow Jobs
banners that spell it amature
who needs Schoolgirl Panties Anal Antics Ungulate Swingers

I want a site that shows only women named Eunice
all of them dressed up to attend PTA
standing before dignified fireplaces
smiling gravely

(well, maybe one of them could wear a jaunty hat)

just thinking about it gets me really hot

Bad Luck

having got her poor heart
broken one more time yet again
she locked her bedroom door
suffered multiple and intense attacks
of logorrhea
and finally committed Gongorism

resulting in a bestselling novel
unoriginally touted as *runaway*

we still felt sorry for her until
it happened seven times in a row

now the townswomen bitch & gripe:
That lamebrain cheesy bastard my husband
treats me so well
I'll never make a dime

I Have Been Waiting for the Word

halophilous to come out of the closet
and reveal what it really is

for years it has been claiming
to mean "salt-loving; growing
or living in a region rich in salt"
but even a cursory glance discovers
it probably means "predisposed
toward saintly headgear" or "lit
from behind with benevolent intentions"
or "aspiring to highest sweetness"

it is a base canard to say
of *inspissated* that it means "thickened
by process of boiling or condensation"
when it so obviously signifies
"oversurfeit with beer during a long bus ride"

sublingual is reputed to mean
situated under or on the under side
of the tongue but it really means
"unable to say anything meaningful
whatsoever" and objects such as boulders
ocean beds and bushes are sublingual

it is time that these words
and many others were outed for
underneath their schoolmarmish exteriors
they are ecdysiasts at heart
and sporting bejeweled G-strings

or none

Let Them Eat Gnotobiote

a marauding band of the Logophagoi
has devoured two of my poems

I'd scrawled them in this same notebook
and now those pages are empty

I don't mind too much the loss
of the greeting-card rhyme though
I'd counted on it for pocket change

but I wish I had my epic back
that cost me some sweat

words can be so dry
Why wouldn't these marauders eat cocido madrileño
and follow up with a wedge of torta barozzi?
my lines must have tasted
better than they sounded

I've learned my lesson:
from now on every poem will contain
a word or two like *xanthrophore*
statocyst   *zymogram*   *somatoplasm*
phyllotaxy   *trypanosomiasis*

if the Word-Eaters can stomach these terms
I will find others more threatening
that will disrupt their peristalsis

oh well   let em graze at will
if they find my stuff appetizing
they must be starving.

A Knight in Shining Armor

that's me all over
though the armor is piled in the corner
while I lie here with the Lady Fleurdelice
the naked sword between us

where did it come from I'd like to know
I busted my sword on a big rock
and told her the Dragon did it

but she produced this one from somewhere
smallish   not real sharp   and said
'Twill serve, Sir Federigo, you know the rules

so I'm lying here chaste but not in thought
restless as the Irish Sea
because no matter which way I turn
this rusty courtlax nips me somewhere
nasty cold thing   I wish it was a goat
turd roasting in the tarpits of Eblis

You know, she says, that was cute
you smashing your sword on that stone
I was afraid you'd hear me laughing
behind my tree   it took you 40 whacks at least

It was a stalwart blade, I said
and cost me a trove to get enchanted

What was it enchanted against?

Rocks

You should get your gold back
from the wizard because look
at this crummy sword here that I found
in a ditch and does its job to perfection

The night is young

Not as young as you think

In a ditch you say

Well Hung

The progress of the Queen of Sheba
was indeed spectacular

infantry in shining armor
lockstep even in that filthy desert

kettledrums and trumpets and tabors
the clever ponies   the elephants richly caparisoned
the leopards in their sapphire collars   more eunuchs
than you could shake a stick at

the Queen Her Majesty borne
by gleaming slaves   the silken curtains parting
for an overwhelming instant to reveal
those eyes dark almonds above the silver veil

the archers following on tall camels

I was over beside a dune
trying to take a private whiz
when the outriders spotted me
and came spurring to take off my head

it was just dumb good luck
she observed me first

The Man Who Thinks

he hears a burglar
rises from bed and blunders from room
to room   clicking on the lights
poking the shadows with a broomstick

no one there

Must have been my Imagination, he says
and rejoins his pillow and lies
all night listening contentedly
as his Imagination roars about
slamming doors   tipping over tables
smashing crockery   swearing at injustice

he smiles beatifically and exclaims proudly,
What an Imagination! maybe
I'll put that sucker to work for me

(but you & I know
it has to be the other way round)

Resolution and Independence

all night long from out of the shadows
that passing headlights thundered against
my bedroom wall the dread Four Horsemen
of Insomnia galloped powerfully upon me

and the first was furious Politics spiky
with armament urging his fatted mare
and speaking in tongues forever unknowable
jingling like coinage as on he flew forward

and the second was Religion char-black
as the flamesnorting stallion he spurred
bony he was with wild eyes sunken
and flourished a brand of smoking scriptures

after these came in scarlet all silken
his mare's hooves lisping over the greensward
the third rider Sex of seeming fair aspect
but dangerous to men as the firebelching cannon

the fourth was grimvisaged Literary Critic
his eager lance leveled at all and sundry
he howled a war cry of Marxian Theory
and bore down upon me with no friendly intention

how sorrowfully then I regretted the table
with all its clarets tidal within me
and all its sauces warring one another
and all my inanities vivid in memory

in darkness I lay then sweating and groaning
till I heard from outside the delicate clipclop
of cheerful Aurora on her little gray burro
undertaking to climb the ascendant new day

inspirited I flung off all of the bedclothes
hastened to finish my scanty ablutions
found in the fridge my Budweiser breakfast
and fed to the shredder my novel-in-progress

My Reinvention of the Peach

was a perfect disaster
purplish black little spheroid
as crunchy and bitter as a gallstone

likewise my rose   colorless
sickly and disheveled and so fragile
it shattered like a Christmas tree ornament
even the thorns were pointless

let us not dare to mention
my olive   my quartz pebble
my willow   robin   cornsnake
feather rootlet raindrop violet

and now the President has appointed me
to sit on the Supreme Court of the U.S.A.
and expects me to mete out human justice
impartial to one and all   me
the guy who couldn't even build
a daisy

A Thanksgiving Invitation

freely imitated from the

ELEVENTH SATIRE OF JUVENAL
AND RESPECTFULLY DEDICATED

to

Mr. & Mrs. Stuart Dischell

by Fred Chappell

No one gives a damn if Rockefeller
Squanders ten million bucks on his wine cellar,
But neighbors fall into an awestruck trance
Observing Wastrel's proud extravagance.
His champagne bills go up, his stocks go down;
He makes himself the laughingstock of town.
On his horizon a rainbow future gleams;
He puts his trust in shady pyramid schemes.
Impoverished by bottle blondes in bars,
Instead of dealing, he'll soon be stealing cars.
The bookie and the brothel straitly bind him;
His creditors know always where to find him.
At Chez Pierre he's careful to be seen,
Engorging, like a python, haute cuisine.
Fifty bucks for a sautéed onion:
As onions go, it *was* a paragon;
A true gourmet would find the price a waste,
But Wastrel thinks it must enhance the taste.

Is it not pointless to know the sciences,
While helpless to repair household appliances,
And tell to what the national debt amounts,
But not your savings from your checking accounts?
Know thyself, to set your mind at ease,
Was the advice of canny Socrates:
You may belong to a more modest station
Than flitting off to Palm Springs for vacation.
Thousands to grand opera aspire
Who screech like peafowl in their Baptist choir.
Find where you're headed; march along that track
And you'll avoid the shame of crawling back.

Why does he mortgage for a Lamborghini,
His secret repasts ketchup on a weenie?
Stomp the accelerator; hang the cost—
All his fortune blows out his exhaust.
He pawns his furniture and silverware
To cuddle balls in silken underwear.
One jaunt to Vegas and his estate is sold:
Does he imagine he shall not grow old?
Death, to most, is chiefest of our fears;
To Wastrel, it's the coming on of years.

You'll find, when payment on his loan falls due,
He reimburses by skipping out on you.
Send your attorney to batter at his door;
You'll find he doesn't dwell there anymore.
He thinks no more of reneging on his debt
Than of changing sweat socks when they're wet.
Why should he hang around to face the end?
A new town beckons and a fresh girlfriend.
A herd of debtors flees this town's confines,
Pursued by creditors like starving lions;
When loan sharks and their victims have departed
This busy city stands well nigh deserted.

But now, my dear Dischells, this festive night
You'll find out if ole Fred's a hypocrite,
A scribbler who enjoins modesty,
While shunning such responsibility,
Who preaches moderation as moral law
While pigging out on pheasant and foie gras.
What Fred and Susan have prepared between us
Means you'll dine with Horace, not Maecenas.
For openers we'll mound a wicker tray
With salad greens and wild mushroom paté.
Our entree Susan put together solo,
Lamb shanks marinated in Barolo
And paired off with the cannellini bean:
A rustic staple of the Florentine.
For fruit, a cantaloupe or honeydew,

A Red Delicious, and *une poire d'Anjou.*
Dessert has been a topic of debate—
Almond meringues or a chèvre plate?
I guarantee the potables will shine:
In peaceful protest, we imbibe French wine.

This modest meal President Jefferson
Would smile his heartiest approval on:
Not drenched with sauces no one can pronounce,
No caviar at untold bucks per ounce,
Not served on 18-carat dinnerware—
Old-fashioned, never ostentatious, fare:
A simple meal that in our former days
Would heap a blushing farm wife with warm praise.
From field and garden she would gather viands,
The freshest and the ripest, for her friends,
Wash and drain them, set the pot to boil,
Dress greens with vinegar and peanut oil,
Husk the corn and, with the water hot,
Plunk tender ears into the bubbling pot.
Such were the meals that fed our ancestors
Before this Age of American Emperors.
In those stout times the lack of luxuries
Taught country folk how common things must please:
A well-oiled rifle and a lure well tied,
The white bull calf that was the daughter's pride.

Good times: when war with Germany or France
Was not the hobby of bought presidents.
Religious times: when piety was seen
In church and not the television screen;
Village ministers led the heartfelt prayer,
Not teleranters with their bouffant hair.
Simple times: when handy furniture makers
Would borrow the cleanly designs of Shakers,
Not plundering Honduran mahogany,
But fashioning the useful red oak tree.
Past times: that shall not come again until
Lawmakers regain a long-lost skill

And turn once more to sturdy common sense
When they debate our national defense,
And study closely when they come to vote
The documents that our forefathers wrote.

I've told what we shall offer: Now I list
A catalog of things to be dismissed:
No slide show of a European tour
That vexed a different country every hour,
With Susan wearing pink toreador pants
Or shorts at which the natives look askance,
With Fred standing glass-eyed before the Eiffel,
A deer spotlighted for a poacher's rifle.

We'll skip those pornographic videos
With housewives aping the techniques of pros,
Instruction tapes that graphically define
Three hundred different ways to 69,
And films that star a penis of such size
It bonks its owner square between the eyes.

The walls will sport no head of boar or panda
That I dispatched in China or Uganda,
And no dust jacket in a gilded frame
Of some past book that never verged on fame;
Likewise, no shelf or table shall display
Obscure awards no one recalls today.
We'll share no gossip about Poetry Stars
Or names of poor Jim Dickey's favored bars.
We shall not grouse about our salaries
Which one year more are subject to a freeze;
We shall not jaw about the stupid farces
Of House and Senate crammed with horses' arses.
Such comportment signifies the rich;
The plusher that they thrive, the more they bitch,
Achieve a silly, specious brilliance,
As dopes with manicured insouciance.
They hold it dull vulgarity to save;
They wear Versace to a pauper's grave.

We'll entertain ourselves with memories
Of worthy poets and bright histories;
We'll pull down well-thumbed books and read a bit,
Until our weary spouses bid us quit;
We'll talk of kin and children, friends and pets,
What one remembers and how one forgets;
How some professors drove their points home
And how we nodded off, attending some;
If Musial or Mays was the sharper batter—
We'll lull Thanksgiving Day with placid chatter.

With our Thanksgiving feast let us put by
The routine irritations we decry
And number days that fluttered pleasantly
Through Anno Domini 2003;
Remember the blue, birdsong days of spring,
Count birthdays dancing round us in a ring.

The neighborhood lies quiet as a shroud
As men to television football crowd,
So that their family Thanksgiving Day
Takes place in San Francisco or Green Bay.

I'll tell you, Stuart, what I'm grateful for:
This day comes once a year and never more;
We feast with careful moderation—still,
One always feels he might be falling ill;
Few shall avoid contagion of excess
In a bloat nation sickened with success.

Let's you and I, before this Day is gone,
Pour one last glass of Château Haut-Brion
And raise a toast to patriots of yore
Who fought the just and necessary war.
And now, next door, my neighbor's shout arose;
Someone scored a touchdown, I suppose.
Thick thousands hold our country stands unwell
Until one team gives another hell.

Lazarus

Death is what they call "traumatic,"
i.e., it is no picnic
and I cannot bring myself to speak
of it in detail, but if you imagine
that everything inside your torso,
guts roots, ribcage trunk, heart crown,
is a tree being twisted out by hurricane winds,
and the pain and the void-black fear
coming over you like a deluge of asphalt,
you shall have a dim inkling,
except for the visions that rise howling
but do not reveal their true shapes.

That was the order of my death
and I had not supposed it would be easy.

But then I was brought back
out of the pitiable dark
to the pitiless light,
bones burning like iron bars
in my shriveled stinking flesh,
the green pallor my skin,
my eyes unseeing in the sun,
my shadow always larger than my body.

The disgust you feel at my aspect
I feel one thousand times more deeply.
The horror I inspire in you
is magnified in me and does not abate.

And in ten years or sooner
I must do the dying all over again.

Something to look forward to.

Listen Up, Evildoers Everywhere, Now

that I have my secret credentials
from the FBI, CIA, and NSA
I will be on your ass like crankcase oil
on Gomer Pyle

no crime so horrid that I shall blench
no misdeed so small I shall not note
no conspiracy so complex I shall not unskein
no motive so black I shall not pour
upon it the light of TRUTH

I am studying cryptography
practicing my fast draw
speaking foreign languages
learning to talk real mean

e.g., "Think you're pretty cute, doncha,
wise guy well we've got a special deal
for guys that think they're cute"

I'm coming after you and not just me alone
I'm enlisting my brother Jeb
gonna get him secret credentials too

I have saved an extra boxtop

Quintus Tells Me He Was Born

too late

no use my saying, Q old fellow
you'd be miserable without
your broads bars baseball
your hours would each be separate
and abiding torments

still you maunder on
about how the plain and wholesome life
is best where you would contentedly chaw
potatoes pintos and pone
and sip from the crystal spring 'neath
the picturesque willow

you'd be drably disappointed
what flows from that spring is
water

my man, if I were you
I'd lengthily reconsider
before I ever tried to milk
a warm-teated goat on a frosty morn
or followed with a bulltongue plow
a gnarly-witted dyspeptic mule

the Golden Age is the Land of Youth because
there they all die young
and not from surfeit of pleasure

"You have been observed

coming out of the"
whatever

in the whole squealing horde
this dream is the most frightening

the voice that emits the sentence
precise authoritative toneless
disinterested   without emotion

yet the sense of threat is as palpable
as the taste of a pistol muzzle

there is no face or figure conjoined
the voice sufficient unto itself

Where have I been that I have been guilty?
What secrets harbor that I know nothing of?

anyone might claim
to know you better than you know yourself
but those words always ring false

yet now I wish I could remember
every place I have ever been
everything that I have ever said
the names of those who could have seen
me coming out of the

I would get back at them somehow

The Biography of the Enemy

reveals that his parents were murdered
by the regnant party when he was five
thereafter brought up amid stony pastures
by kindly illiterate goatherds

his sisters raped and beheaded
when he was twelve

when he turned sixteen the explosion
at the 12th Sector munitions dump
went unproved against him

then he disappears
until at age nineteen he enrolls
at Oxford to read classics
and write on Thucydides

many young men discuss Thucydides
that in itself is not suspicious

but this fact when mounted
with other pieces of intelligence
(his reverence for the hard cheeses
of his native hills   his distaste
for American cinema   his premature
condemnation of theodicy
and later recantation   his longing
to master the Debussy etudes)
compose a picture not comforting in the least

these things we know and many others
we've followed his career for decades
can identify his foreign allegiances
and track most of his known associates

yet cannot say where he met his wife
the beautiful corrosive Rosamunda
or when the lower provinces began
to hail him as a revolutionary saint

his connection to the suicide
of his father's brother is tenuous at best
his influence with the massed troops
on the eastern border conjectural
our administration stoutly denies
that he could have masterminded
the North Central Station bombing

we keep him under tightest surveillance
and can assure every citizen
he is no immediate threat

last year we almost found out his name

All of Us Are Everywhere

and none of us is anywhere

you are in a place, inside the car itself
but also in other places as you roll
through the town not acknowledging these
as places because there seems no attachment
you shall never boast that you have conquered
the whole 1300 block of Sycamore Ave.,
shall never say of it, "I was the man,
I traveled, I was *there*"

then your destination toward which
you project your thoughts, being *there*
in a certain limited sense, as well as at the scene
you left behind on 14th St.
and now recall with dampish regret

that's not the half of it

because you are also anxiously talking to Roberta
on the cell phone and see her in your head twisting
the way she does the receiver wire
around her wrist as she denies being where
she was when you claim she was

and also listening or half listening to the radio
which places your mental image of yourself
in a rapt auditorium where the crooner sang
of some place he was not but pretended
to desire to be, in this case Abilene

it is not just you but all of us
in so many different places at the same instant

What wonder divorce is rampant?

Deep in the Heart of Texas

the man with two brains
decided not to wear a hat

but then changed one of his minds
and pictured a bowler maybe
an umbrella to underscore its sobriety

his other mind was steadfast
imagined a shaven head
a leather jacket with oodles
of chains zippers snaps studs

that was only the start soon
one brain preferred the American league
the other the National   one thought
time antedated space the other
the opposite   one blondes   one redheads
democrat republican   light dark

the two brains never lit
upon the idea of compromise
and were always in painful conflict

then they proposed that separate
living quarters might provide relief
and so foraged about and acquired
another head from a perfect stranger

then followed a trial with death
sentence and an eventual lethal injection

and the voices were silent at last

Man Bites Dog

they tell me is a newsworthy story
but why is that since Man Bites Just About Everything
is the facts of the case and the canine race
cannot hope to be exempt
from such wholesale mordacity

Dog Bites Man is decidedly unnewsworthy
unless Dog makes a mortal job of it

then all Sheol breaks loose
lawsuits in flashbulb courthouses
with Dog claiming Man bit him first
and the humans handwringing and sternly
over and again growling *Bad Dog!*

hard to know which is worse:
nature when you tamper with it
or when left unleashed

better to avoid the quarrel
and house two kittens instead
one of them named Eugenia
the other possibly Beatrix

Man Bites Cat
now that would be a story

Hello Once More

I am Fred's answering machine

you would not have dialed this number again
unless you had dialed many others
and were disappointed with their answers

so now I will tell you the secret
of the universe and save you further bother

here it is:

you may wish to find pencil and paper

a time will come when it is no longer time

no I don't understand it either but then
I don't have to

I got it from the Delphic Oracle
who is the Mother of all answering machines

don't call here again